SPOTLIGHT ON POETRY
Classic Poems

Contents

Collected by Brian Moses and David Orme

Acknowledgements

Whilst every effort has been made to contact the copyright-holders and to secure the necessary permission to reprint these selections, this has not proved to be possible in every case.

'A Slash of Blue' by Emily Dickinson, reprinted by permission of the publishers and the Trustees of Amherst College from *The Poems of Emily Dickinson*, Thomas H. Johnson, ed., Cambridge, Mass., USA. The Belknap Press of Harvard University Press, Copyright ©1951, 1955, 1979, 1983 by the President and Fellows of Harvard College. 'Macavity: the Mystery Cat' by T.S. Eliot, from *Old Possum's Book of Practical Cats* by T.S. Eliot, reprinted by permission of Faber and Faber.

Published by Collins Educational
An imprint of HarperCollins*Publishers*
77–85 Fulham Palace Road
Hammersmith
London W6 8JB

www.**Collins**Education.com
On-line support for schools and colleges

© HarperCollins*Publishers* 1999

First published 1999

Reprinted 2000

Reprinted 0 9 8 7 6 5 4 3

ISBN 0 00 310 332 3

All rights reserved. No part of this publication may be reproduced, stored in a retrieval system or transmitted in any form or by any other means – electronic, mechanical, photocopying, recording or otherwise – without the prior written permission of the Publisher or a licence permitting restricted copying in the United Kingdom issued by the Copyright Licensing Agency Ltd, 90 Tottenham Court Road, London W1P OLP.

Designed by Clare Truscott
Cover Design by Clare Truscott and Kate Roberts
Illustrations by Tim Archbold, Phillip Burrows, Louise Drake Lee, Maureen Galvani, Emma Garner, Patricia Linnane, Melanie Mansfield, Katty McMurray, Holly Swain, Stephen Waterhouse, Sue Williams

Printed and bound in Hong Kong by Printing Express

Collins Educational would like to thank the following teachers and consultants who contributed to the research of this series:

Mrs J. Bibby (St Paul's C of E Primary); Jason Darley, Liz Hooley (Jessop Primary School); Mrs M.G. Farnell (High Meadow First School); Alison Lewis; Chris Lutrario; Lesley Moores (Princess Royal Primary School); Sheila Stamp (Castle Lower School); Sally Prendergrast (Brooke Hill School); Jenny Ransome; Jill Walkinton; Sue Webb; Michael Webster (Castle Lower School); Jill Wells (St Andrews CE Primary School).

Evening Star

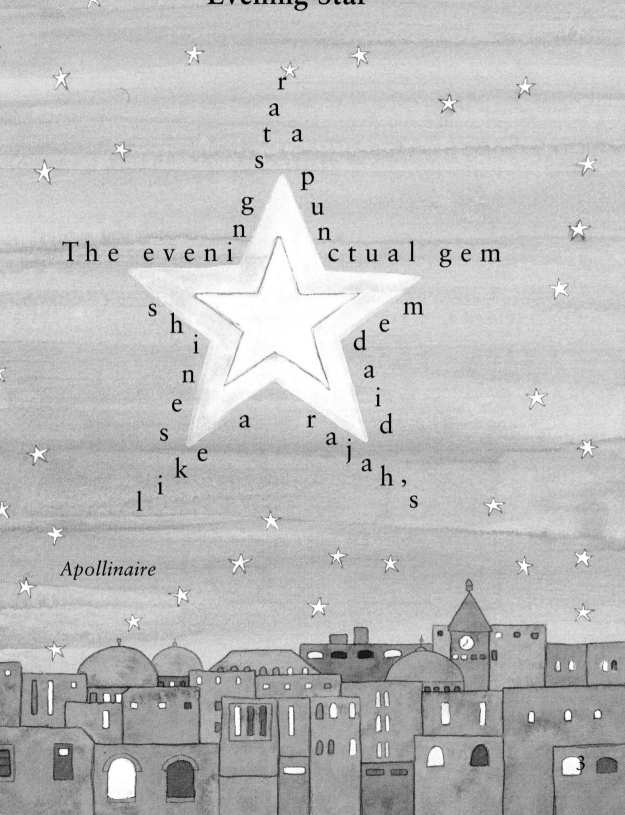

The evening star, a punctual gem,
shines like a rajah's diadem

Apollinaire

3

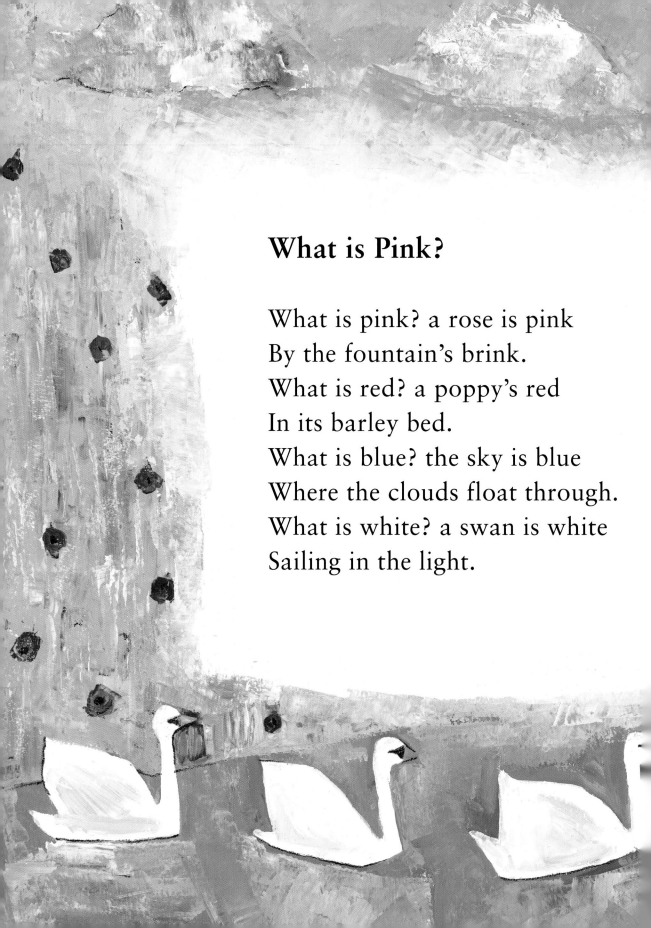

What is Pink?

What is pink? a rose is pink
By the fountain's brink.
What is red? a poppy's red
In its barley bed.
What is blue? the sky is blue
Where the clouds float through.
What is white? a swan is white
Sailing in the light.

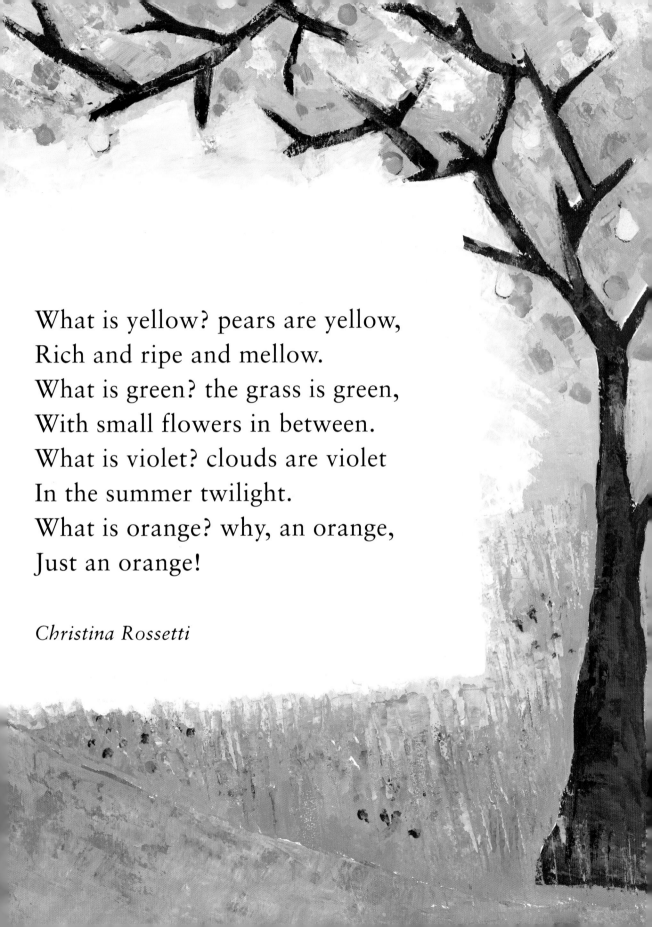

What is yellow? pears are yellow,
Rich and ripe and mellow.
What is green? the grass is green,
With small flowers in between.
What is violet? clouds are violet
In the summer twilight.
What is orange? why, an orange,
Just an orange!

Christina Rossetti

A Riddle

There is one that has a head without an eye,
    And there's one that has an eye without a head.
You may find the answer if you try;
    And when all is said,
Half the answer hangs upon a thread.

Christina Rossetti

Leg Riddle

Two legs sat upon three legs
With one leg in his lap;
In comes four legs
And runs away with one leg;
Up jumps two legs,
Catches up three legs,
Throws it after four legs,
And makes him bring back one leg.

Traditional

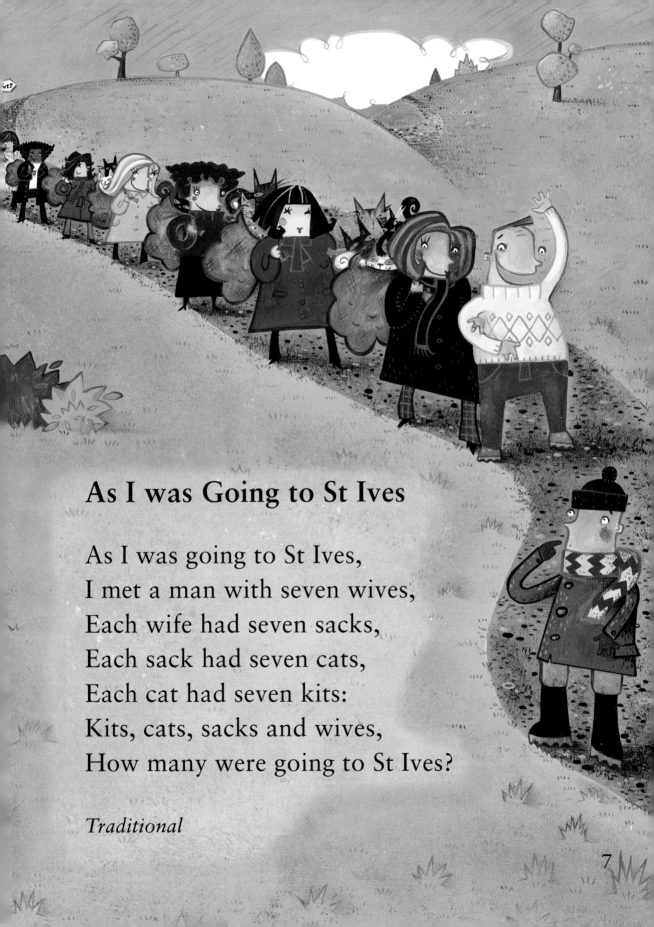

As I was Going to St Ives

As I was going to St Ives,
I met a man with seven wives,
Each wife had seven sacks,
Each sack had seven cats,
Each cat had seven kits:
Kits, cats, sacks and wives,
How many were going to St Ives?

Traditional

A Slash of Blue

A slash of Blue –
A sweep of Gray –
Some scarlet patches on the way,
Compose an Evening Sky –
A little purple – slipped between
Some Ruby Trousers hurried on –
A Wave of Gold –
A Bank of Day –
This just makes the Morning Sky.

Emily Dickinson

How Doth the
Little Crocodile

How doth the little crocodile
Improve his shining tail;
And pour the waters of the Nile
On every golden scale!

How cheerfully he seems to grin.
How neatly spreads his claws,
And welcomes little fishes in,
With gently smiling jaws!

Lewis Carroll

The Months

January brings the snow,
Makes our feet and fingers glow.

February brings the rain,
Thaws the frozen lake again.

March brings breezes loud and shrill,
Stirs the dancing daffodil.

April brings the primrose sweet,
Scatters daisies at our feet.

May brings flocks of pretty lambs,
Skipping by their fleecy dams.

June brings tulips, lilies, roses,
Fills the children's hands with posies.

Hot July brings cooling showers,
Apricots and gillyflowers.

August brings the sheaves of corn,
Then the harvest home is borne.

Warm September brings the fruit,
Sportsmen then begin to shoot.

Fresh October brings the pheasant,
Then to gather nuts is pleasant.

Dull November brings the blast,
Then the leaves are whirling fast.

Chill December brings the sleet,
Blazing fire, and Christmas treat.

Sara Coleridge

The Storm

See lightning is flashing,
The forest is crashing,
The rain will come dashing,
A flood will be rising anon;

The heavens are scowling,
The thunder is growling,
The loud winds are howling,
The storm has come suddenly on!

But now the sky clears,
The bright sun appears,
Now nobody fears,
But soon every cloud will be gone.

Sara Coleridge

Windy Nights

Whenever the moon and stars are set,
    Whenever the wind is high,
All night long in the dark and wet
    A man goes riding by.
Late in the night when the fires are out,
Why does he gallop and gallop about?

Whenever the trees are crying aloud,
   and ships are tossed at sea,
By on the highway, low and loud,
   By at the gallop goes he.
By at the gallop he goes, and then
By he comes back at the gallop again.

R. L. Stevenson

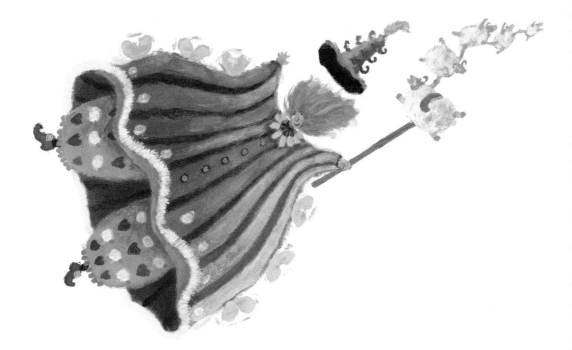

The Wind

Who has seen the wind?
    Neither I nor you;
But when the leaves hang trembling
    The wind is passing through.

Who has seen the wind?
    Neither you nor I;
But when the trees bow down their heads
    The wind is passing by.

Christina Rossetti

A was an Apple-Pie

A was an apple-pie;
B bit it,
C cut it,
D dealt it,
E eat it,
F fought for it,
G got it,
H had it,
I inspected it,
J jumped for it,
K kept it,
L longed for it,
M mourned for it,

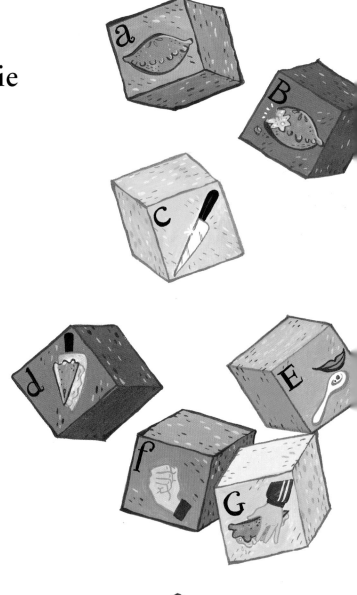

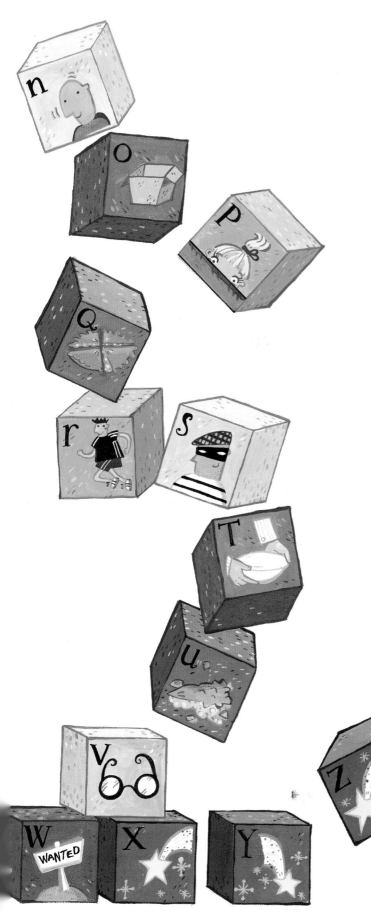

N nodded at it,
O opened it,
P peeped in it,
Q quartered it,
R ran for it,
S stole it,
T took it,
U upset it,
V viewed it,
W wanted it,
X, Y, Z and
    ampersand
All wished for
    a piece in hand.

Traditional

Gulliver in Lilliput

From his nose
Clouds he blows.
When he speaks,
Thunder breaks.
When he eats,
Famine threats.
When he treads,
Mountains' heads
Groan and shake;
Armies quake.

See him stride
Valleys wide.
Over woods.
Over floods.
Troops take heed.
Man and steed;
Left and right.
Speed your flight!
In amaze
Lost I gaze
Toward the skies:
See! and believe your eyes!

Alexander Pope

The Sleepy Giant

My age is three hundred and seventy-two,
     And I think, with the deepest regret,
How I used to pick up and voraciously chew
     The dear little boys whom I met.

I've eaten them raw, in their holiday suits;
     I've eaten them curried with rice;
I've eaten them baked, in their jackets and boots,
     And found them exceedingly nice.

But now that my jaws are too weak for such fare,
    I think it exceedingly rude
To do such a thing, when I'm quite well aware
    Little boys do not like to be chewed.

And so I contentedly live upon eels,
    And try to do nothing amiss,
And I pass all the time I can spare from my meals
    In innocent slumber – like this.

Charles E. Carryl

The Spider and the Fly

'Will you walk into my parlour?' said the Spider
     to the Fly,
''Tis the prettiest little parlour that ever you
     did spy;
The way into my parlour is up a winding stair,
And I have many curious things to show when
     you are there.'
'Oh no, no,' said the little Fly, 'to ask me is
     in vain,
For who goes up your winding stair can ne'er
     come down again.'

'I'm sure you must be weary, dear, with soaring
up so high;
Will you rest upon my little bed?' said the Spider
to the Fly.
'There are pretty curtains draw around, the sheets
are fine and thin;
And if you like to rest awhile, I'll snugly tuck
you in!'
'Oh no, no,' said the little Fly, 'for I've often
heard it said,
'They never, never wake again, who sleep upon
your bed!'

Mary Howitt

Macavity: The Mystery Cat

Macavity's a Mystery Cat: he's called the
    Hidden Paw –
For he's the master criminal who can defy the Law.
He's the bafflement of Scotland Yard, the Flying
    Squad's despair:
For when they reach the scene of crime –
    Macavity's not there!

Macavity, Macavity, there's no one like Macavity,
He's broken every human law, he breaks the law
    of gravity.
His powers of levitation would make a fakir stare,
And when you reach the scene of crime –
    Macavity's not there!
You may seek him in the basement, you may look
    up in the air –
But I tell you once and once again,
    Macavity's not there!

Macavity's a ginger cat, he's very tall and thin;
You would know him if you saw him, for his eyes
    are sunken in.
His brow is deeply lined with thought, his head is
    highly domed;
His coat is dusty from neglect, his whiskers
    are uncombed.
He sways his head from side to side, with
    movements like a snake;
And when you think he's half asleep, he's always
    wide awake.

Macavity, Macavity, there's no one like Macavity,
For he's a fiend in feline shape, a monster
    of depravity.
You may meet him in a by-street, you may see
    him in the square –
But when a crime's discovered,
    then Macavity's not there!

He's outwardly respectable. (They say he cheats
    at cards.)
And his footprints are not found in any file of
    Scotland Yard's.
And when the larder's looted, or the jewel-case
    is rifled,
Or when the milk is missing, or another Peke's
    been stifled,
Or the greenhouse glass is broken, and the trellis
    past repair –
Ay, there's the wonder of the thing!
    Macavity's not there!

Macavity, Macavity, there's no one like Macavity,
There never was a Cat of such deceitfulness
    and suavity.
He always has an alibi, and one or two to spare:
At whatever time the deed took place –
    MACAVITY WASN'T THERE!

And they say that all the Cats whose wicked
　　deeds are widely known
(I might mention Mungojerrie, I might mention
　　Griddlebone)
Are nothing more than agents for the Cat who
　　all the time
Just controls their operations: the Napoleon
　　of Crime!

T. S. Eliot

Glossary

Evening Star

punctual   on time

rajah   Indian prince

diadem   jewel worn on
the head

What is Pink?

brink   edge

mellow   sweet

twilight   evening, when
it is getting dark

A Slash of Blue

compose   make

How Doth the Little Crocodile

doth   old-fashioned
word for 'does'

Nile   important river
in Africa

The Months

fleecy dams   mother sheep

posies   bunches of flowers

gillyflowers   wallflowers

sheaves   bundles

borne   carried

pheasant   a bird bred for
shooting

The Storm

anon   soon

Windy Nights

by on the highway   along the
road

A was an Apple-Pie

dealt   gave out

mourned   felt sad because
someone had died

quartered   cut into four parts

ampersand   &

a piece in hand   a slice
of apple pie

Gulliver in Lilliput

famine   hunger

treads   walks

quake   shake with fear

troops take heed
soldiers take notice

steed   horse

30